NATIVE AMERICAN MYTHOLOGY

FRED RAMEN

rosen publishing's
rosen central®

New York

Published in 2008 by The Rosen Publishing Group, Inc.
29 East 21st Street, New York, NY 10010

First Edition

Library of Congress Cataloging-in-Publication Data

Ramen, Fred.
Native American mythology / Fred Ramen.—1st ed.
    p. cm.—(Mythology around the world)
Includes bibliographical references and index.
ISBN-13: 978-1-4042-0738-7
ISBN-10: 1-4042-0738-4
1. Indian mythology—North America. 2. Creation—Mythology. 3. Tricksters—United States. 4. Indians of North America—Folklore. 5. Tales—North America. I. Title. II. Series.
E98.R3R37 2007
398'.4108997—dc22

                                                                2005035283

Manufactured in the United States of America

On the cover: This Navajo sand painting is of a Yei god, a class of deity in the Navajo pantheon. Sand paintings were traditionally used in healing and blessing ceremonies.

CONTENTS

INTRODUCTION

One very cold day a young boy went out hunting with his bow and arrows. He was a good hunter and shot several partridges. He turned back through the woods to bring them to the village, but the snow was very deep and he grew tired. He decided to stop and rest next to a huge stone that resembled a human head.

As he sat next to the stone idly chipping a piece of flint, he heard a deep voice speak suddenly, shaking the trees around him with its power: "I will now tell a story."

"Who said that?" asked the boy.

"I am Hahskwahot," said the voice. "I am Great Stone. I shall tell a story."

The boy realized that it was the stone itself that was speaking to him!

"First leave me one of your birds," the stone said. The boy placed one of his partridges on the rock, and Great Stone began to speak again. It told him a wonderful tale of how the world had begun when Sky Woman fell to earth and the Great Turtle caught her and formed the land. When the story was done, the boy returned to his village and told the people the story he had heard. For a while they forgot the cold of winter and shared the joy of the tale with each other.

The next day the boy returned to Great Stone with another partridge. He gave it to the stone and Hahskwhahot told him another legend. This is how it went for many days; the boy learned about magical animals and strange forest spirits, of great heroes and battles in the sky and on the earth. With each story, he returned home and shared it with his family and the people of the village.

One day, when the boy had become a man, he returned to the stone. "I have told you all my stories," said Hahskwhahot. "You now have the legends and will pass them to your children. Now that there are stories in the world, more stories will be added. And wherever you go you will be welcomed and fed, as it is right to do to the storyteller. I have spoken."

And so it was that Native American myths came into the world.

An Iroquois "false face" mask appears above. These carved wooden masks are used in healing ceremonies and represent mythological beings whose help is requested for curing the sick. They are carved directly into tree trunks and removed from the tree when completed.

This charming Iroquois story is an excellent introduction into the world of Native American mythology. In it we can see many details of how these people told their stories—and more important, how stories like this one were central to their way of life. The story-teller commands respect, and an offering must be given to him as a token of respect. Native American stories are magical in nature and are revealed to humans by spirits of great power. Thus storytelling is not just something to while away time; it is an act of worship that strengthens the bonds of the community.

But before we hear more stories of the Native Americans, we must learn about who these people were, and where and how they lived.

1 THE WORLD OF NATIVE AMERICANS

Like all early inhabitants of North America, the people we call Native Americans arrived from elsewhere in the world. Unlike Americans who arrived in North America from Europe, however, Native Americans migrated from Asia.

Nearly every aspect of the history of Native Americans is intensely controversial, from simple questions about how many were living in North America when the Europeans first arrived, to when the Native Americans themselves

This nineteenth-century doll made of wood, sinew, and teeth by Yup'ik Indians of Alaska represents a shaman's spirit helper. By putting him in contact with the spirit world, the helper enabled the shaman to heal the sick.

How Many Were There?

The arrival date of the Native American people in North America is not the only controversy about their history. For many years, historians and anthropologists have been arguing about how many Native Americans lived in North America before the coming of the Europeans.

For a long time, it was believed that North America was very sparsely populated at the time of the European "discovery." The usual estimate, first calculated at the beginning of the twentieth century, was that there were approximately one million people living on the continent when Christopher Columbus arrived. That number was based on the size and number of Native American tribes observed during the eighteenth and nineteenth centuries.

However, there were problems with this reasoning. The early Spanish invaders in the Caribbean and Mexico reported populations in the millions. For a long time, these numbers were thought to be an exaggeration. However, recent historical research has uncovered evidence that the population of North America may have been much higher than previously thought.

It is well known that diseases, such as smallpox and measles, brought by the Europeans were the biggest killers of Native Americans, who, having never encountered these illnesses before, had no immunity to them. By studying church and government records, researchers determined what percentage of the infected Native American populations usually died, and then compared it to the number of deaths actually recorded. Using this method, they determined that the population of North America was much higher—perhaps between 8.5 and 15 million people—with millions more in Mexico. The lower populations in the nineteenth century were the result of these massive pandemics that wiped out so many people.

first reached the Americas. Most historians agree on the broad outlines of their story, however.

Long ago, during the period we call the Ice Age, the earth was much cooler than it is today. Huge glaciers—great masses of ice and snow—covered much of present-day Canada and northern Europe. Because ice takes up more space than water, the sea level was lower in those days than it is today. This allowed people from Asia to cross into North America on foot.

Scientists believe that the Bering Strait—the narrow body of water between Alaska and Russia—may have been dry land during the Ice Age. (Some feel that it was not completely dry, but that it had enough small islands that people in tiny boats could cross the water without ever being far from land.) It is not known for certain when the first people came across the "land bridge" named Beringia; most estimates are between 12,000 to 18,000 years ago. Recent evidence, however controversial, has emerged that may indicate humans reached the Americas as early as 30,000 years ago.

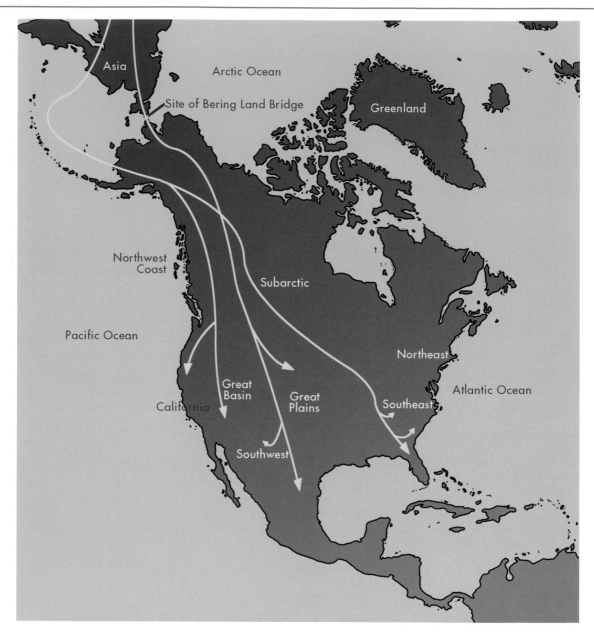

The likely migratory routes various tribes took from Asia before settling in North America are outlined in this map. The peoples who would become known as "Indians" or "Native Americans" crossed what would have been a land bridge at the present-day Bering Strait, which separates Alaska from Russia.

These early immigrants to North America quickly migrated from Alaska to inhabit every part of the Americas. For example, the Inuit settled in the Arctic Circle regions of what is now present-day Canada, and the Yamana settled in Tierra del Fuego at the tip of South America. Wherever Native Americans settled, they adapted their society to meet the demands of the climate. In so doing, they created cultures that had a remarkable degree of harmony with their environment.

Although they remained a Stone Age people, the Aztecs of Mexico and the Incas of South America were brilliant gold- and silversmiths. Yet they never made iron or even bronze tools. Still, both groups left behind artifacts of remarkable sophistication. The Aztec pyramids in Mexico are well known, as are the great stone cities of the Incas in Peru, but few people know of Cahokia, a large Native American city in present-day Illinois. Now in ruins, this great city was once home to more than 30,000 people around the year 1100; more people lived there than in Paris, the capital of France, at that same time.

The Native Americans lived in harmony with the natural world, but they also altered it to improve their lives. Many visitors to the Amazonian rain forest are astonished that there are so many fruit trees teeming with food. What they don't realize is that these trees were planted thousands of years ago by the Native American inhabitants of the forest. When the English colonized the region we call New England, they noted with wonder how broadly spaced the trees were in the forest—with gaps wide enough to drive a carriage through; this was also the work of the Native Americans who had

An eighteenth-century rock drawing found in Arches National Park in Utah depicts a deer hunt. In the American Southwest, there are typically two types of Native American rock art found: petroglyphs (images scratched onto a rock surface) and pictographs (images painted onto rock with dyes and pigments).

lived there. They had carefully tended the forests to make them the perfect place for deer, their primary source of meat, to survive.

Cultural Distinctions

Because of the very distinct environmental regions of North America, various tribes living in neighboring areas had similar cultures, sharing many of the same customs, tools, and even myths. The following are the main cultural regions of Native North Americans.

Pomo Indians of northern California crafted this basket made of clamshell disks, glass beads, woodpecker and quail feathers, and tree materials. Pomo baskets in earthen hues of black, tan, and dark brown are considered among the best crafted, strongest, and most beautiful in the world.

Pacific Northwest

The tribes of the Pacific Northwest, such as the Tlingit, are famous for their totem poles and intricately carved masks. The rugged mountains and forests of the region provided them with the materials to make wooden vessels in the form of dugout canoes. With the ability to make these small vessels quickly and easily, many became excellent navigators, and they paddled around the coastal region, trading with other tribes. Eventually they became noted for their highly developed trading practices.

California and the Great Basin

The Great Basin—the mountainous, arid region of what is now Utah, Nevada, Wyoming, and Colorado—was once inhabited by nomadic people like the Utes and the Shoshone. These tribes and others like them managed to survive in an inhospitable land by gathering seeds and hunting small game. Although California is not part of the Great

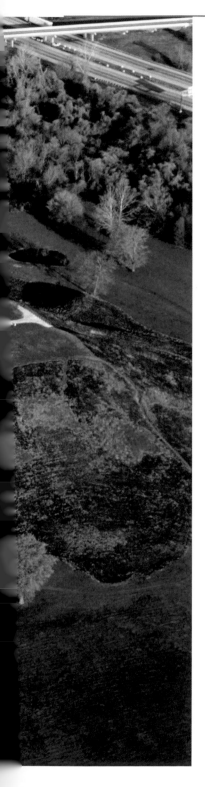

Basin, its people shared cultural similarities with the Basin people; they were noted for their ability to turn acorns into food.

The Plains

When most people think of Native Americans, they think of the tribes of the plains, such as the Sioux, Cheyenne, and Crow. Originally from the eastern part of America, the people of these tribes became nomadic hunters when they moved onto the plains. After the Europeans brought horses to North America, the Plains Indians became renowned for their ability to hunt and fight on horseback.

The Southwest

The tribes of the Southwest lived in large adobe (sun-dried brick) structures, called pueblos,

The raised earthen surface in this photograph is known as Monks Mound. It is located in Illinois and is believed to have been a central part of Cahokia, a large city that may have served as a cultural and spiritual center for Mississippian Indians. Cahokia probably included large public plazas and buildings, temples, playing fields, and satellite villages. What purpose the Monks Mound site served—temple, ceremonial platform, public building—is as yet unknown. It was abandoned by the Mississippians in the fourteenth century but remains North America's largest human-made earthen mound.

Where Did They Live?

Most people think of the tepee, the conical tent of buffalo hide, when they think of the kinds of houses in which Native Americans lived. Actually, each Native American tribe developed its own unique housing system tailored to the weather conditions of the local climate.

In the Pacific Northwest, the tribes made houses out of wooden planks with pitched roofs, much like the houses most Americans live in today. There was no chimney, however, just a smokehole, and an entire family lived in each house, which was up to 70 feet (21 meters) long.

In the Northeast, the Iroquois were famous for their wooden longhouses. These houses were made of wooden frameworks covered in bark and could be up to 200 feet (61 meters) long. Each house was inhabited by a clan, or large group of related families, and was divided into sections where each family lived around its own fire.

In the Southwest, the Pueblo and Dine tribes lived in large houses of adobe. Each house was connected to the others, and each family lived in its own rooms, much like a modern apartment building. In the basement of each building was a sacred space where the men of the tribe would hold religious ceremonies.

The nomadic tribes of the Great Plains lived in tepees. They were ingeniously designed: the tent was held up by between ten to fifteen poles made of saplings, with an open top to allow smoke to escape. An interior lining of hide created a continuous flow of air. Thus people inside the tepee could cook around an open fire, keeping themselves warm in the winter. Easy to put up and to take down and very portable, the tepee was the perfect shelter for the wandering tribes of the plains.

A palace complex built into the side of a cliff by the Pueblo Indians is one of the most stunning attractions at Mesa Verde National Park in Colorado. The park includes 600 cliff dwellings built between 600 and 1300 CE. They were made of sandstone, mortar, and wooden beams, and may have originally been painted with plaster.

which resembled modern apartment buildings. They were very successful farmers of corn, even in the arid regions of Arizona and New Mexico. This area was also once the home of the Anasazi, a pueblo culture that had built a remarkable civilization with many large cities before disappearing in the 1300s.

The Southeast

This region was once home to the descendents of the Mound Builder cultures that had built Cahokia; they lived in large, well-planned and fortified towns. They were devastated by diseases spread by the Europeans, and their culture collapsed in the 1500s.

The Eastern Woodlands

The tribes of the Eastern Woodlands—the Hurons, the Iroquois, the Abenaki, and others—lived in large villages made up of wooden longhouses, each one the home of several families from one clan. The Iroquois were actually a federation of five separate tribes. Each tribe had its own democratic government and controlled much of present-day New York State.

All Native American tribes share a cultural and mythological heritage. In this book, we will examine four different types of stories that nearly all Native Americans told. These include creation stories, which tell about how the world came to be; animal stories, which explain why animals must be respected; trickster stories, which tell about a clever animal who manages to escape by using its wits; and hero stories, which tell about how tribal leaders helped their people survive and founded the traditions by which they live.

2 CREATION MYTHS

All cultures have a story, or creation myth, that explains how the world began and how they came to be in it. The Native Americans are no exception. Their creation myths are notable for two reasons: the stories explain how people came to this world from some other, magical place, and they detail a close cooperation between animals and humans. The following creation myth is from the Iroquois, the great confederation of Eastern Woodlands Indians whose method of government influenced the writing of the United States Constitution.

The nine clan animals of the Cayuga nation—a member of the Iroquois confederation—stand on the Great Turtle's back in this twentieth-century sculpture by Cayuga artist Wayne Skye. The animals are the hawk, snipe, wolf, beaver, turtle, eel, deer, heron, and bear.

Sky Woman

Long ago there was no land anywhere in the world, only a deep ocean. Far above the waters, however, there existed a place called Skyland, where the Sky People lived. Their chief, an ancient and magical man, had a young wife who was about to give birth. One night she had a dream, which she told to her husband the next morning. She had dreamed that the tall, beautiful Great Tree that grew in the center of Skyland had been pulled up. Her husband heard the story and said, "This is a dream of power. We must make it true."

He gathered the young men of Skyland together, and they pulled and tugged at the tree until finally the chief himself pulled it out of the ground.

Iroquois "false face" masks are considered to be living and are "fed" tobacco and hot corn mush. The false faces have special powers over the winds, bad luck, illnesses affecting the joints and shoulders, toothaches, earaches, swelling, and nosebleeds. Anyone who is healed through the use of such a mask is invited to join the False Face Society, a curing society.

Through the hole it left they could see far down, through the sky to the distant waters below. As the young woman looked in the hole, she suddenly lost her balance and fell through it. She tried to grab a branch to stop her fall, but her grip slipped and she kept falling, clutching some seeds in her hand.

Two swans saw her falling. "We must help her," they said, and flew up and caught the Sky Woman, but they could only slow her fall.

The animals in the water were worried. "She cannot swim," they said. "How will she survive here?"

"We must dive for the earth that is beneath the waters," said one of the water birds. First Duck tried, but he could not reach the bottom. Beaver and Loon tried as well, but both failed. Finally, little Muskrat dove. She swam and swam until her lungs nearly burst, but she reached the bottom and took one small paw of mud back to the surface.

"Put it on my back," said the Great Turtle, who had come to see how he could help. Muskrat climbed on his back—and today on the backs of turtles, you can still see where she scratched his shell. As soon as she put the mud on his back, the pile of earth began to grow until it became all the land in the world. Then Sky Woman landed on the new ground and planted her seeds. From those seeds grew all the trees and grasses and other plants of the world. Life on earth had begun.

In this story, we see how the world begins in goodness, with harmony between humans, animals, and plants, as well as the divine origin of human beings. In the next myth, a story from the Dine or

Navajo peoples of the Southwest, we see not only the creation of the world, but a warning about how it can end.

Four Worlds

This world is not the first world that was created. The First World existed far below this world. In that world, there was no light. In that darkness were six people: First Man, First Woman, Fire God, Salt Woman, Coyote, and Begochiddy, the son of the Sun. Begochiddy was neither male nor female but both; he had golden hair and deep blue eyes.

Begochiddy began to make things in the world. He made four mountains—white, blue, yellow, and black. He made insects and the first plants. But things did not go right in the first world. The six people did not like the darkness, even after Fire God

Part of the Navajo creation myth is depicted in this nineteenth-century blanket based upon a sand painting design. In it, the First Man and First Woman flank a maize plant. The First Man and First Woman were said to have emerged from ears of white and yellow corn and were taught by the Mountain People of the Third World how to plant corn and build homes.

started to set the world on fire. To improve the world, Begochiddy had them gather together all the plants he had made. A Big Reed grew, and the First Beings climbed inside it as it ascended into the sky, growing taller and taller until the six original people came to the Second World.

The Second World was all blue. There were people there, Swallow People and Cat People, but the First Man fought them off. Begochiddy made more things in the Second World; he made the clouds and more plants and mountains. For a time they were happy there, but after a while they tired of the Second World as well. Perhaps they had begun to fight. However it happened, Begochiddy summoned the Big Reed again, and the group rose up in it to the Third World.

The Third World was yellow, and it was the most beautiful of the worlds they had seen. The mountains of the Third World glowed brightly, so although there was no sun or moon, the world was still filled with light. Begochiddy filled this world with many beautiful things, and everything was in harmony. Then he made the men and women.

At first everything went well. But then things worsened. Diseases struck the men and women. They began to quarrel with each other, each sex blaming the other, until Begochiddy separated them on different sides of a great river.

This brought peace for a while, but the men and women became unhappy without each other. Begochiddy united them again but warned them that the world would be destroyed if they again caused trouble among themselves.

Coyote, meanwhile, wandered the world, as he liked to do. One day, Salt Woman told him about a strange thing she had seen at a place where two rivers flowed together: a baby with long black hair floating in the water. Coyote went to the rivers and took the baby from the water.

Within a few days, the Water Buffalo woman started a mighty storm because she was angry that her baby had been taken. Begochiddy knew that she was going to flood the world, so he called up the Big Reed again. The people rose up on it, but this time it did not reach the next world. The Spider People wove a web to attempt to guide them to the next world, but they could not break through it. The Ant People tried to burrow to the Fourth World, but they failed as well. Finally, Locust, with his hard head, succeeded in making a hole into the next world.

The Fourth World was filled with water, but the powerful beings who lived there caused the waters to recede. "Who will dry the ground?" asked Begochiddy. Badger tried, but he sank in the mud. That is why today all badgers have black paws from the mud of the new world. Then the winds came and blew the land dry.

Still the waters of the Third World continued rising. As they did, they threatened to flood the Fourth World through the hole Locust had made, until Begochiddy made Coyote open his blanket, revealing the Water Baby where he had hidden it. They dropped the baby through the hole and the waters receded.

The Fourth World is our earth. Begochiddy made the stars, the moon, the sun, and many other things. Coyote stole fire from the Fire God and gave it to humans, and then Begochiddy taught them how

A silver, leather, and turquoise Navajo wrist guard, circa 1930, is based upon the wrist guards known as ketohs worn by ancient Navajo archers to protect their forearms from the snap of the bowstrings. This allowed them to shoot off arrows more accurately and for longer periods of time before becoming chafed, fatigued, or injured.

to grow beans, corn, and squash. Begochiddy also taught them how to live in peace and harmony with the natural world. This myth teaches that this world will also be destroyed if people forget themselves and stop living the right way.

In this creation myth we see the importance of living in harmony with one another and the natural world, which was created in a state of balance. If people upset this balance, it can destroy the world as they know it. This need for balance and harmony is a key feature in many Native American stories. Animals play an important role in both creation stories. In the next chapter, we will examine other myths where animals play central roles.

3 ANIMAL MYTHS

Native Americans told many stories about the animals in their world. Both the animals Native Americans hunted for food and the animals they used for labor, such as dogs and horses, played a huge part in everyday life.

But animals represented more than just food and assistance to the Native Americans, who studied animals and how they behaved not just to learn how to hunt them, but to learn how to live in harmony with nature. To Native Americans, animals were more than just creatures who lived in the wild; they were also messengers from the spirit world. And just like people all around the world, Native Americans used stories about how animals behaved to teach important lessons in how humans should behave.

Tlingit and Haida dancers would dress in elaborately carved and painted masks and hats—like this eagle hat—that represented creatures of the natural and mythical worlds.

Animal myths were also used to explain how creatures had come to look the way they do today. The first myth in this chapter is an Iroquois story that not only explains how the buzzard came to have no feathers on his head, but also offers an important lesson in learning when to be satisfied.

How Buzzard Got His Feathers

Long ago, when animals and birds could still talk, the birds had no feathers. They were ashamed to have nothing to wear, so they hid from all the other animals until they could take it no longer. All the birds in the world met in a great council and decided to send one of them to fly to the Creator and ask him for clothes to wear.

Buzzard was chosen because he could fly the highest of all the birds on his long wings. He set out immediately for the sun-place, where the Creator lived. He flew and flew for a long time. The food the other birds had given him had run out, so he circled down when he saw some fish lying on the ground. He was so hungry that he stopped and ate the rotten fish, even though it smelled awful.

After he ate, Buzzard kept flying, getting closer to the sun until his head was burned red with the heat. But at last he reached the sun-place where the Creator met him.

"I have been waiting for you," the Creator said. "I have heard the prayers of the birds and made you all fine suits of feathers. Because you have been so brave and flown so high, you may choose your suit first. You can try on any of these suits, but you may only try them on once."

An eagle feather headdress that once belonged to Yellow Calf, a chief of the Arapaho Indians, appears above. The Arapaho lived on the eastern plains of Colorado and Wyoming after migrating from the areas of present-day Minnesota and North Dakota. Yellow Calf was the last traditional chief of the Arapaho. His headdress is made of both fur and feathers.

"Thank you, Grandfather," said Buzzard. He tried on many different feathers, but none suited him. Goldfinch's feathers were too yellow; Blue Jay's too blue; Cardinal's too red. He tried on suit after suit of feathers, but none seemed appropriate.

Finally Buzzard put on an ugly brown suit. Unlike the other suits, it did not change its size to fit him—it remained too small. His legs stuck out from the bottom, and his neck and burned head were left completely bare. "This is the worst of all of them," he said.

"Ah, Buzzard," said the Creator, "it is the last suit left. You have made your choice."

And so it is to this day. Buzzard still eats things that have been dead for a long time because that's what he did on his long trip, and he still wears the poorly fitting clothes he earned by being too picky. But he remains proud because he alone of all the birds was able to make the trip. And when he is riding high in the sky, circling the sun, he is the closest of all the animals to the Creator.

Native Americans respected the animals with which they shared their world. Perhaps because of this, there are many stories of people who went to live with animals, taking on their characteristics and even becoming animals themselves. Many of these stories are about people who lived with bears, who were admired for their great strength and skill as hunters. Bears can also seem almost human at times. Living alone in the deep woods and high mountains, they must have been attractive symbols of the power, mystery, and harmony of the natural world.

The next myth is adapted from the Tlingit people of the Alaskan panhandle and tells the story of one human who went to live with bears.

The Bear's Wife

One day a young Tlingit girl was walking through the woods, carrying a heavy basket of salmon, when she nearly stepped in a pile of bear droppings. Stumbling to get out of the way, she dropped her basket and scattered her fish all around. She was so upset that she said many mean things about bears and their ways, even though she had been taught not to do so.

Some time later, on a summer morning, the girl was collecting berries near a stream when a slight movement caught her eye. A tall, handsome man with broad shoulders and the powerful grace of a wild animal emerged from the woods. "I have come to make you my wife," he said. And so she went with him.

He did not live like the Tlingit did, in a house made of wooden planks, but in a dark cave in the woods. The man treated her well and brought her many good things to eat. In return, he made only one demand his wife. He asked that she not turn to look at him until the sun was over the horizon.

For several weeks she followed his command, but one day her curiosity got the better of her. Pretending to sleep, she watched as her husband awoke one morning. What she saw shocked her. Instead of a man, a great grizzly bear sat up beside her! It shuffled to the front of the cave and then shrugged off its fur, revealing her

The Tsimshian tribes of northern British Columbia and southern Alaska are composed of clans named after animals—Wolf, Raven, Eagle, Killer Whale, Bear, etc. The clans are arranged hierarchically, meaning some are more prominent and have a higher status than others. The Bear Clan is one of the most important ones. This mask was probably worn by a dancer of the Bear Clan.

husband. He was the bear she had insulted before, and he had taken her away from her people to punish her for wronging bears.

That winter they slept together in their cave den, and she had two sons. When the spring came, they all went outside to play. Her sons put on bearskins and pretended to be bears like their father. But the girl was unhappy. She wanted to return to her people and began to plot for ways to bring her brothers, who were great hunters, to her aide.

But bears have powerful magic, especially the ones who can change into human beings. Because of these powers, her husband knew of her plans. He told her, "After your brothers have killed me,

Totem poles are usually carved from towering red cedar trees. The carved figures running up and down the pole can represent figures from myths and legends, clan lineages, or historical tribal events. They can also serve as tomb markers, with grave boxes built into them.

they must sing these songs and perform these rites that I will teach you in order to summon my spirit into the afterlife. They must do that for all bears, whenever they kill one."

And so it was. The girl's brothers and their dogs soon found her husband in his bear form, and he did not attack them but let them shoot him dead with their arrows. The brothers found the girl, whom they thought was dead, and brought her and her sons back to the village.

It was hard to adapt to life among human beings again; her sons were used to the smell of bears, not people. The next spring, the girl's littlest brother begged her to let him practice hunting. "Let my nephews dress up in their bear skins, and I will shoot them with my toy bow." The girl resisted for a long time, but eventually she gave in.

The little brother got too excited, though, and began to use his real arrows, shooting them one after another at the little boys. Enraged, the girl turned to confront him—and at that moment she turned into a huge grizzly herself. She struck him down with her paw and fled with her children into the woods. Later, the people in a nearby village saw a bear and two cubs heading away from the lands of people. They had lost the ability to become human again. But the people remembered the lessons of the girl, and whenever a bear was killed they said the appropriate rites, so that bears and people can continue to live in harmony.

Native Americans also had other kinds of animal stories. We call them trickster stories because they involve animals that use their wits—not their strength—to survive and often delight in playing tricks on other animals.

4 TRICKSTER MYTHS

Many cultures throughout the world have had stories centered on characters who like to play tricks on other people, and who survive by their wits and nerve rather than through their strength. In other cultures, trickster myths often feature humans or gods. The Norse god Loki, for example, is a trickster in some myths. In Native American culture, however, tricksters are often animals. Although various animals can be tricksters, they are often fast-moving, small creatures

A 1,500-year-old petroglyph of a rabbit appears above. It was etched into a rock on a limestone cliff near Hamilton Dome in Wyoming. The site contains over 250 such petroglyphs, including those of birds, buffalo, elk, deer, antelope, mountain sheep, bears, turtles, dogs, and lizards.

who are excellent at disguising themselves or hiding. The rabbit is frequently a trickster in both Native American and African stories, as are the fox and the skunk. The trickster tradition is alive and well in modern storytelling as well. The cartoon character Bugs Bunny is a notable modern trickster, a fabulous descendent of the rabbit stories of the original Americans.

The first story in this chapter is from the Iroquois and features a rather unique trickster, a turtle. He is unique because he is so much slower and smaller than other animals and must therefore be smarter than them to survive. In this story, which has similarities to the famous fable "The Tortoise and the Hare" by the Greek author Aesop, Turtle outwits Bear to win a race.

Turtle Races Bear

Long ago when animals could talk, Bear was out walking grumpily in the snow. In those days, he did not spend the winter sleeping, though he did not like the coldest season. He came to the edge of a pond covered in ice. Turtle stuck his head up through a hole in the ice and greeted Bear. "Hello, friend!"

"Greetings, Slow One," said Bear. As the most powerful of the animals he had a high opinion of himself and often put on airs.

"Why do you call me slow one, oh Bear?" asked Turtle.

"Why, it should be obvious," said Bear. "You are small and slow, while I am the great Bear, greatest of the hunters, most powerful animal in the world. If we were to have a race, I would surely beat you."

"Then let us race," said Turtle, who did not like Bear thinking so much of himself. "We will run to the end of the pond, you along the banks, and I under the water."

"How will you do that?" said Bear. "The ice covers the pond."

"I will cut many holes in it tonight. When I reach each hole, I will stick my head through it, so you can see who is winning the race."

And so it was. The next morning many of the other animals gathered to watch the race. As soon as the sun was the height of a hand above the horizon, it began.

Bear took off at a fearsome pace. But no sooner had he started than Turtle's head popped out of the next hole in the ice. "Here I am, Bear, try to catch up!"

Bear ran even faster, but almost immediately Turtle appeared at the next hole. "Here I am, Bear!" And so it kept happening: the faster Bear ran, the quicker Turtle's little head appeared, shouting "Try to catch up, Bear!"

By the time Bear reached the finish line, Turtle was already there receiving praise from the other animals. Bear was so tired and ashamed that he went off into a cave and slept there until the spring, just as he continues to do today.

But after all the other animals had left, Turtle knocked on the ice. At each of the holes in the ice, a turtle's head appeared! "Thank you, cousins! We have taught Bear not to look down on the other animals, and all the other animals know that turtles are not slow, either!"

In the Iroquois story, Turtle teaches Bear a lesson—but more than that, he is able to win because he can see the weakness in his

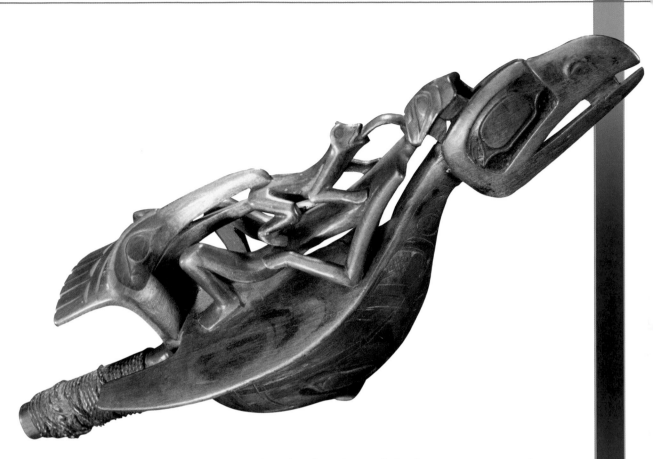

A Tlingit rattle made of carved and painted wood depicts a raven carrying a reclining human, a frog (sitting on the human), and a long-billed bird at the raven's tail. For the Tlingit peoples, the raven was a trickster and a transformer. It was seen as both benevolent and mischievous as illustrated by its stealing of daylight from heaven and bringing it to a previously darkened world.

opponent. Bear is foolishly proud and thus falls for a simple trick. Many trickster stories follow this pattern, where the trickster escapes because his opponent is too confident or focused on one thing (like eating the trickster!) to escape the trick before it is too late.

Other trickster stories, however, involve the trickster himself getting fooled or beaten because of his own overconfidence. Such stories probably served as a way to keep people from trying to get away with tricks too often, since deceit could be bad for the community.

In this Pawnee story from the Great Plains, Coyote—one of the most famous tricksters in Native American mythology—fails to show the proper respect to anyone and comes to a bad end.

Coyote and the Rock

Coyote was out hunting. It had been a long time since he had caught anything, and he was very hungry. He came across a large rock on top of a hill. "Grandfather," he said to the rock, "I give you my flint knife. Help me catch something to eat."

He left the knife on the rock and went down the hill. At the bottom of it he found a freshly killed buffalo. "At last some food!" he said. "But I need a knife to cut up the buffalo."

He went back up the hill and took his knife off the rock. "You won't need this," he said to the rock. But when he reached the bottom of the hill, the buffalo was gone; all that remained were some old bones.

Suddenly, there was a rumbling noise. Coyote turned around, and then started to run. The rock was rolling down the hill after him! He passed some bears. "Help me, bears!" he shouted. But they shook their heads. "We can't help you against Grandfather Rock." He passed some mountain lions. "Help me, lions!" he shouted. But they shook their heads, too. "Nobody can help you against Grandfather Rock."

The Plains Indians greatly admired the wolf for its strength and endurance, its hunting skill, its ability to work within a group, and its tendency to share food with members of its pack. This wolf mask and headdress is being worn during a powwow. Wolf masks would also often be worn during hunting expeditions.

He passed some buffalo. "Help me, buffalo!" he shouted. "We'll help you!" said the buffalo. They stood in the rock's path and lowered their heads to catch it, but the rock smashed through them and crushed their heads against their bodies, just as they appear today.

All the while, the rock kept rolling faster and faster, gaining steadily on Coyote.

High above, some nighthawks were flying. "Hey, nighthawks," shouted Coyote, "this rock that's following me says you are a bunch

of ugly birds with eyes that are too big, mouths that are too wide, and pinched-up beaks."

The leader of the nighthawks was furious. He and his brothers and cousins and friends attacked the rock with their beaks, breaking it into smaller and smaller pieces until it was just a pile of gravel. Coyote stopped and laughed.

"Well, Grandfather, how strange," he said disrespectfully. "Did those ugly pinch-beaked, big-eyed wide-mouthed birds do this to you?" Then he laughed again and started off on his way.

The leader of the nighthawks had heard him, though. He and his people fanned the pile of little stones

To the Tlingit peoples, owls were ominous and terrifying creatures. Children were made to behave and stop crying with warnings that owls would come and take them away if they didn't remain quiet and well-mannered. Adults believed owls talked but only delivered bad news. This carved and painted Tlingit statue is an "owl-man" with prey clutched in its sharp claws.

together with their wings. The next thing Coyote knew, he heard the rock following him again—and before he could get out of the way, it rolled over him and flattened his body.

Tricksters are important characters because they are able to break the rules of the society, allowing people to think about what it would be like to break those rules. But cultures need more than tricksters—they need heroes who uphold their society's highest ideals and aspirations. The next chapter introduces some of the great heroes of Native American mythology.

5 HERO MYTHS

All cultures have heroes, the people who display the virtues that society values and respects. Moreover, heroes are part of the creation story of that culture. Myths about heroes explain why people must follow certain rules and why heroes are considered the founders of that culture's society.

In many cultures, the hero can also be a trickster, or at least have many of the same qualities as the typical trickster. However, the hero can often rely on more than just his wits. Heroes are often great warriors or hunters and can frequently employ the use of powerful magic.

Gluscabi is one such hero-trickster. The Abenaki of present-day New

The Great Plains Indians known as the Shoshone created this painting of a buffalo hunt and ceremonial dance. The painting is applied directly onto an animal hide. The Buffalo Dance was held before a hunt and was designed to praise the buffalo's spirit and encourage a herd to pass nearby the hunters.

England believed he was the first man in the world. Gluscabi made himself from dust that Tabaldak, the Creator (his name means "the Owner"), brushed off of his hands after he had made the world. Gluscabi is strong and clever but often gets into trouble because he does not understand that the world is carefully balanced and must remain in harmony.

Gluscabi Goes Hunting

Gluscabi went out hunting one day, but the animals saw him coming and hid. He could not catch any of them and came home angry because he had nothing to eat.

Gluscabi lived in a little lodge at the edge of a great lake with Grandmother Woodchuck. "Make me a game bag," he asked her. (A game bag is a sack or pouch a hunter keeps the animals in that he has caught.) Grandmother Woodchuck made him all kinds of bags, but Gluscabi rejected them all. Finally, she offered to make a bag out of woodchuck fur. She plucked the fur off of her own belly, which is why woodchucks have no fur there today.

This game bag was magic. No matter how much you put inside it, there was always room for more. Gluscabi went out into the woods. "Animals, listen, the world is going to be destroyed!"

"Help us, Gluscabi!" said the animals. "What can we do?"

"Come hide inside my bag," he said. At his request, all the animals in the world came and hid inside his bag. Then he tied it up and came home to Grandmother Woodchuck.

An Inuit bag appears above. Inuit are Native peoples who live in the Arctic regions of Canada, Greenland, Alaska, and Russia. Bags like this could be used for gathering, carrying, and storing game and other food, as well as tobacco, pipes, paint, medicine, trinkets, and tools. The material was usually tanned leather, rawhide, bird skins, buckskin, wool, grass, bark, fiber, or as in this case, fur. This bag's ivory handle, and others like it, were intricately carved with geometric designs.

He showed her the bag. "Look, Grandmother, we'll never have to hunt again." Grandmother Woodchuck looked inside. All the animals in the world looked back at her.

"Oh, Gluscabi," she sighed, "this is not the right way. The animals cannot live inside your bag. They will all die, and then there will be none left for your children, or their children. It is right for it to be hard to catch them. In doing so, you will become stronger. The animals in turn will become harder to catch and there will always be balance."

"You are right, Grandmother," said Gluscabi. He took the game bag back into the forest and opened it up. "Animals, come out," he said. "The world was destroyed, but I put it back together again. Go back into the woods." And they are there today because of the wisdom of Grandmother Woodchuck's words.

Gluscabi is a hero not only because he possesses great cunning, but because he does the right thing. He provides an example to his people by hunting responsibly. He also offers an explanation for why it is important to keep a balance in the natural world.

The Cheyenne tale of Motzeyouf is an example of another kind of hero—one who has great power, uses it to help his people, and establishes the very rules of his society.

Arrow Boy

Long ago there was a young orphan among the Cheyenne of the Great Plains. His name was Motzeyouf, or Arrow Boy. From the day he was born, he showed that he had great powers. He could make buffalo appear or disappear, and he performed many other magical deeds. One day, the old medicine men of the tribe invited him to dance for them. Motzeyouf tied a noose around his own head and had two men pull on each end while he danced. Suddenly the noose tightened, and his head rolled clean off of his shoulders. His body fell to the ground, but in an instant he was standing up whole

Cheyenne warriors wore colorful shirts made of hide that was painted and decorated. Decorated panels ran across the shoulders, below the neck opening, and along the tops of the sleeves. This shirt is decorated with porcupine quillwork embroidery. The fringe on a warrior's shirt could be made of human or animal hair, buckskin, or ermine.

again. In this way, he demonstrated that he was the greatest of the medicine dancers.

The next day, the tribe caught some buffalo. Motzeyouf went out to where the animals had been killed because he wanted a buffalo hide. He wanted to make a new robe since his old one was tattered and falling apart. Young Wolf, the chief of the tribe, who everyone feared because he ruled through the force of his cruel warriors, came upon Motzeyouf and demanded the buffalo hide. Motzeyouf refused to give it to him, and when Young Wolf tried to take it, he hit the chief in the head with a buffalo hoof, killing him.

Young Wolf's warriors sought out Motzeyouf, but he had hidden from sight, using his ability to change into different animals in order to hide. For five days he appeared before the warriors, but they could never catch him. Each appearance, however, was in the costume of one of the four warrior societies of the Cheyenne: the Red Shields, the Coyotes, the Elks, and the Dog Warriors.

After this, Motzeyouf wandered far away to the Black Hills. There he found a mountain with a door in the side. He entered through this door, and he found himself in an enormous lodge. Around a council fire were gathered different people from all over the world: red, black, brown, and white. They had come to learn the secrets of the world from the Great Medicine (a Cheyenne god who created the sun, moon, stars, earth, and its oceans). Motzeyouf stayed with them for four years learning how to become a prophet.

Meanwhile the Cheyenne were starving. They could not catch any buffalo and were reduced to eating mushrooms and herbs. One day, some boys were digging in the ground for roots. They saw a

A late nineteenth-century drawing by a Southern Cheyenne depicts a mounted Indian hunting a buffalo with bow and arrow. Cheyenne women also took part in buffalo hunts by driving the buffalo toward the men, who shot them with their bows.

man approach them. "Bring me some buffalo bones," he said. They did so, and he folded the bones into his robe. When he opened the robe, the bones had turned into meat. With this development, they knew that Motzeyouf had returned.

Motzeyouf stayed with the people for a long time. He showed them four arrows he had brought back from the holy mountain and taught them the songs to sing over them. When he had finished the fourth song, the buffalo herds came thundering by the lodge. He reminded the people to kill only as many as they needed to survive.

Motzeyouf founded the five warrior societies. He told the people that they must never let a cruel chief control them as Young Wolf had done. To ensure a balance in law, he created the council of forty chiefs and the four warrior chiefs.

When he was very old, Motzeyouf made a final prophecy. "Beware the light-skinned strangers," he said. "They will bring sicknesses of all kinds to you. Their gifts will be wonderful at first but will make you forget all the people who have lived before you. They are restless and cruel, and will hunt for yellow stones and kill those who keep the stones from them. They will not be satisfied with killing only what they need . . . [and] they will turn the whole world into stone . . ." After that Motzeyouf vanished and was never seen again. But the Cheyenne still keep the four holy arrows that he gave them and follow all the ways that he preached.

A Shoshone engages in a ritual dance. Shoshone ceremonies often feature dances. These include the Butterfly Dance (a woman's dance celebrating the renewal of life), the Prairie Chicken Dance (celebrating the bird's mating season and the beginning of new life), the Owl Dance (a social dance for couples), the Rabbit Dance (in thanksgiving for its fur and meat), and the Sun Dance (which is held every summer and is the year's most important religious ceremony, celebrating the cycle of life, death, and rebirth).

Conclusion

Motzeyouf's prophecy came true. From across the ocean came bearded, light-skinned strangers clad in metal, who spoke languages never before heard among the Native American people.

These strangers profoundly changed the face of North America. Where there had been only villages, now towns and cities emerged. Roads connected these new places, and the forests were cut down to build more buildings and to open up the land for farming.

The strangers at first seemed friendly, but soon they came into conflict with the Native Americans. They fought them with swords or shot at them with bows and muskets. New diseases also appeared wherever the strangers went, and they killed many people—so many that entire tribes sometimes vanished in the span of a few years.

The people took some of the gifts the strangers from across the ocean brought. The horse, the biggest domestic animal they had ever seen, changed the way the Plains tribes lived almost overnight, as did the guns they bought, traded, or took from the strangers. But always there were more strangers and fewer Native Americans. The Native Americans always lost the wars, even when they won the battles.

In the end, the strangers were victorious. They took over the land and lived on it with their new ways. They forced the Native Americans to live like them and forget their old customs. But not everything was lost. Not everything was forgotten. And to this day, the stories of the people—their myths—continue.

GLOSSARY

Abenaki Eastern woodlands people who lived in present-day New England.

animal myth A story about animals (who can often talk). It can explain how they came to look the way they look now or teach a lesson about how to get along with people.

anthropologist A scientist who studies human societies.

Aztecs People who lived in central Mexico and formed a powerful empire with many large cities. They were conquered by the Spanish in the early 1500s.

Cheyenne Plains tribe that ranged from the Dakotas and Montana to Wyoming and Kansas; notable for having several warrior societies, each with their own distinctive style of dress.

creation myth A story explaining how the world began and how people came to live in it.

Dine A Pueblo people of the Southwest, known as excellent silversmiths and turquoise jewelry-makers.

glacier A huge expanse of ice and snow that completely covers the land below it. Glaciers can be as tall as mountains.

ice age A period of time when the earth's ice caps grow and glaciers cover much of the Northern Hemisphere; the last ice age ended about 10,000 years ago.

Incas People who lived on the west coast of modern-day Peru, Ecuador, and Chile. The Incas had a stong empire that was conquered by the Spanish in the early 1500s.

Iroquois A confederation of initially five (and later six) tribes in present-day New York State. They lived in longhouses—in fact, their name for themselves meant "people of the Longhouse."

longhouse Iroquois dwelling; a long narrow building of wood covered with birchbark that could be over 200 feet (61 m) long.

Navajo Another name for the Dine people.

nomadic Lacking a fixed place to live; describes people who wander from place to place.

pueblo A kind of building made of clay bricks resembling an apartment house; used by several tribes in the Southwest.

Tlingit Pacific Northwest tribe who live on the Alaskan panhandle.

trickster A type of hero who survives by using his wits and who likes to play tricks on other people.

FOR MORE INFORMATION

American Indian Movement
Box 13521
Minneapolis MN 55414
(612) 721-3914
Web site: http://www.aimovement.org

American Indian Policy Center
1463 Hewitt Avenue
Saint Paul, MN 55104
Web site: http://www.airpi.org

Institute of American Indian Arts (IAIA)
83 Avan Nu Po Road
Santa Fe, NM 87505
(505) 424-2300
Web site: http://www.iaiancad.org

National Congress of American Indians (NCAI)
1301 Connecticut Avenue NW, Suite 200
Washington, DC 20036
(202) 466-7767
Web site: http://www.ncai.org

Red Earth, Inc.
2100 NE 52nd Street
Oklahoma City, OK 73111
(405) 427-5228
Web site: http://www.redearth.org

Web Sites

Due to the changing nature of Internet links, Rosen Publishing has developed an online list of Web sites related to the subject of this book. This site is updated regularly. Please use this link to access the list:

http://www.rosenlinks.com/maw/naam

FOR FURTHER READING

Alexander, Hartley Burr. *Native American Mythology*. Minneola, NY: Dover Publications, 2005.

Angulo, Jaime de. *Indian Tales*. New York, NY: Hill and Wang, 1953.

Bruchac, Joseph. *Native American Animal Stories*. Golden, CO: Fulcrum Publishing, 1992.

Bruchac, Joseph. *Native American Stories*. Golden, CO: Fulcrum Publishing, 1991.

Bruchac, Joseph. *Return of the Sun*. Freedom, CA: The Crossing Press, 1990.

Caduto, Michael J., and Joseph Bruchac. *Keepers of the Animals: Native American Stories and Wildlife Activities for Children*. Golden, CO: Fulcrum Publishing, 1997.

Erdoes, Richard, and Alfonso Ortiz. *American Indian Myths and Legends*. New York, NY: Pantheon Press, 1985.

Gill, Sam D., and Irene F. Sullivan. *Dictionary of Native American Mythology*. New York, NY: Oxford University Press, 1994.

Joseph, Alvin M., ed. *500 Nations: An Illustrated History of North American Indians*. New York, NY: Gramercy, 2002.

Lake-Thom, Robert. *Spirits of the Earth: A Guide to Native American Nature Symbols, Stories, and Ceremonies*. New York, NY: Plume, 1997.

Leeming, David Adams. *The Mythology of Native North America*. Tulsa, OK: University of Oklahoma Press, 2000.

Mann, Charles C. *1491: New Revelations of the Americas Before Columbus*. New York, NY: Knopf, 2005.

Ortiz, Alfonso, ed. *American Indian Trickster Tales*. New York, NY: Penguin, 1999.

Philip, Neil. *The Great Mystery: Myths of Native America*. New York, NY: Clarion Books, 2001.

Pritzker, Barry M. *A Native American Encyclopedia: History, Culture, and Peoples*. New York, NY: Oxford University Press, 2000.

Waldman, Carl. *Atlas of the North American Indian*. New York, NY: Checkmark Books, 2000.

Waldman, Carl. *Encyclopedia of Native American Tribes*. New York, NY: Facts on File, Inc., 2006.

BIBLIOGRAPHY

Brown, Dee. *Teepee Tales of the American Indian*. New York, NY: Holt, Rinehart and Winston, 1979.

Bruchac, Joseph. *Iroquois Stories*. Freedom, CA: The Crossing Press, 1985.

Caduto, Michael J., and Joseph Bruchac. *Keepers of the Earth*. Golden, CO: Fulcrum, Inc. 1997.

Pelton, Mary Helen, and Jacqueline DiGennaro. *Images of a People: Tlingit Myths and Legends*. Englewood, CO: Libraries Unlimited, Inc., 1992.

■ INDEX

About the Author

Fred Ramen studied English and comparative literature at Hofstra University. He is the author of *The Historical Atlas of Iran*, also by Rosen Publishing, Inc. He maintains a longstanding interest in Asian culture and is a practitioner of the martial art aikido. Ramen lives in New York City and was recently a participant in the *Jeopardy!* Ultimate Tournament of Champions.

Photo Credits

Designer: Tom Forget; **Editor:** Wayne Anderson
Photo Researcher: Amy Feinberg